ORIGIN OF
CASTE IN INDIA

ORIGIN OF CASTE IN INDIA

JT

PARTRIDGE
A Penguin Random House Company

To order additional copies of this book, contact
Partridge India
000 800 10062 62
www.partridgepublishing.com/india
orders.india@partridgepublishing.com

PREFACE

This book is an attempt to present caste in its entirety, in a common relationship with life as is its starting point. For the reason that caste is a part of life and if you dissect life to examine it, what you end up examining is not life.

This book is also an attempt to offer a primer, providing essential information about caste from as many viewpoints as possible. For the reason that most of the books see caste as a collection of impositions having no regard to its life and others see it as abstraction of one's ethics disregarding the many facets of its exterior.

These two endeavors are not clearly delineated so as to enhance the pleasure of seeing one's interest in an entirely different light.

CONTENTS

As Shri Bhimrao Ambedkar says "Subtler minds and abler pens than mine have been brought to the task of unraveling the mysteries of caste; but unfortunately it still remains in the domain of the 'unexplained' not to say of the 'unundersrood'[1a]". Never has this observation been more apt than now, when no aspect of social and political life of India is free of its influence. And this influence seems to be on the rise, notwithstanding the best efforts to the contrary by the state as well as every right thinking entity. To unravel some of the mysteries this institution holds within, let us take a journey through its origin and development.

"Caste", as defined, for example, by Lundenberg[2] "is merely a rigid social class into which members are born and from which they can escape or withdraw with extreme difficulty". In other words, it is a type of stratification system, which is most rigid in matters of mobility and distinction of status. Much need to be explained about the genesis of this system, though a good deal has been written about its nature, especially the various features of control influencing its members, its origins does not seem to have received enough attention. Some of the theories proposed are,

Racial theory—that caste system is a gift of Aryans,

Political theory—that caste system is an invention of Brahmins,

Occupational theory—that caste system is the functional differentiation of occupational differences,

Traditional theory—that caste system is of divine origin aimed to maintain social harmony,

Guild theory—that caste system is the product of interaction between guilds, tribes and religion,

Religious theory—that caste system is the institutionalization of prevailing customs, each caste being the followers of certain deity and

Evolution theory—that caste system is a product of social evolution moderated by various factors, like prejudices, lack of control mechanisms, geographic isolation of Indian peninsula as well as conquerors' policies, especially that of the British, to name a few.

1

THEORIES OF CASTE—
AN EXAMINATION

1.1 Racial Theory: The fact that caste names Brahmana, Kshtriya, and Visya are frequently mentioned in the RigVeda along with words like 'dasa', 'varna', gives credence to the theory that caste is an invention of IndoAryans. In 'cultural history of India' Al Basham mentions that caste system evolved to accommodate large variety of tribes into Aryan society during expansion of vedic Aryan territories.

However, such delineation fails to notice the importance generally was ascribed to 'the moral worth' of a man rather than his 'birth', which, we can see at many places in puranic literature, the life of 'Eklavya' mentioned in 'mahabharata' being one example. Also, such literature does not give much evidence indicating practice of caste differentiation in daily life and demarcation of people on that basis. In Al Baroonis India, he describes human, according to Indian thought, as "consisting of 25 elements, soul

1

(sattva, tamas, rajas), matter, nature, will" etc, learn all these and one "will achieve salvation whatever religion one may follow". Similar is the opinion of Sir Vincent Smith, who in 'Asoka-his History' says "Though each caste has its own dharma, the conduct is less rigid than it has been since Moslem invasions". From all these, a conclusion one can reach is that, caste, as we see now, needs some more explanation, than that, "it has been evolved during intermingling of Indo Aryan local tribes".

1.2 Political Theory: In Mahabharata (shantiparva) creation of caste is given thus: "Brahma created the world entirely Brahmanic. Later, those Brahmins fond of sensual pleasure became kshtriyas. Those Brahmins who subsisted by agriculture neglecting their duties entered the state of Vaisya and those who were fond of mischief and falsehood sank into the condition of Sudras"[1b]. In 'Hindu Caste System ....'[3], Dr Sharma explains the formation of caste thus: To meet liturgical needs, the society from among themselves would select, on the basis of skills of elocution, the Brahmins. Similarly, for administrative purposes, those with qualities of leadership would be selected ... Furthermore, visha(clan or tribe) also embodied people known as Shudra (meaning not of tribe, newcomers) representing all new comers to that particular tribe .... Thus all responsibilities related to a visha could be grouped into four subcategories", each having "their duties and skills". Though caste can thus be seen as having been a useful tool for maintaining social order, the more or less vicious form it now maintains needs much more explanation than what is offered by this theory.

1.3   Occupational theory: According to 'Theodosian' code, in early Roman Empire, son was required to follow fathers' profession, thus maintaining availability of skill while solving the question of continuation of enterprises. That such an arrangement was widely followed can be observed in many of the popular surnames of today, Smith, Miller, Potter, to name a few. How these occupational guilds and other family groups metamorphosed into castes, in India, while they amalgamated fully into the larger social canvas in rest of the world, is a question, needing sharper wits and greater efforts perhaps, to answer.

1.4   Traditional theory, Guild theory and Religious theory: These theories propose divine intervention in human affairs. Such intervention regulates society by maintaining harmony in all essential functions necessary for social well being, mankind being left free in search of bliss. Occupational groups, which originate as a result of such harmony, on passage of time, happened to convert themselves into castes, readily so, as they were following endogamy. In this phenomenon of caste formation, some groups find themselves becoming endogamous and others find themselves forced into becoming so by society (by closing all avenues of social interaction). Such a theory may be able to explain the formation of castes as a singularity in social evolution, but fails in providing rationale for the continued existence of the vast expanse of castes and related observances, each more irrational than the other, in Indian society.

1.5 Evolutionary theory: This hypothesis, in fact, is not an altogether new or different theory. It states, in effect, that over the years, formation of caste is influenced by all factors we have seen earlier, in one form or other.

2

DEVELOPMENT OF CASTE—
A STUDY

2.1 The origin and development of caste system therefore narrows down to the distinctiveness, of evolution of Indian society which could cause the natural variations existing among its constituents to transform into a more hardened form, under their influence in ancient India. The stratification property of caste, one such peculiarity, in fact is not a monopoly of India. Its mention can be found at many places, like, history by Herodotus, Mande or Osu caste systems of Africa. These, the division of people into four estates in medieval Europe, of feudal barons, clergy, urban merchants and the mass of people as well as the grouping among old Israel population having ritual ramifications are a few places where one can find established systems of differentiating humans to varying levels.

Such a process of division, in fact, has been a subject of study by sociologists, notably, Herbert Spencer, who in his sociological theories have put forth following generalizations:

- The larger the number of people and internal transactions, greater will be the size and degree of internal differentiation of government.

- The greater the actual or potential level of conflict with other societies and within a society, the greater will be the degree of centralization of power in a government.

- The greater the centralization of power, the more visible class divisions will be and the more these divisions create actual or potential conflict.

Like colonies of all living species, powerful leadership and consequently concentration of power did happen in all cultures giving rise to class structures.

2.2 Thus we see, though the tendency to form social class is present in every society, in our case, the stratification became increasingly stable, crystallizing into castes. The main factor which effected this transformation, of a social class into a caste, is another custom which slipped into Indian society, endogamy. Says Ambedker "Remember that endogamy is foreign to the people of India . . . It is no exaggeration to say that with the people of India exogamy is a creed and none dare infringe it . . . there are more rigorous penalties for violating exogamy than there are for violating endogamy. Castes, as far as India is concerned, means superposition of endogamy on exogamy". He further elaborates how, sati or enforced widowhood (where widow is not allowed to remarry), imposition of celibacy on widower as well as girl marriage came to be part of Indian "uxorial customs to maintain numerical parity between the two sexes", making endogamy workable leading to perpetuation of caste system.

2.3   S Charles Hill says "Instead of allowing ourselves to be misled by the outward show of Hinduism we must concentrate our attention on what the Hindu writings tell us . . . According to the Bhagawat Gita, to be truly wise one must have learnt:

- To control the body in its appetites and desires so that it does not injure itself or impede the free action of soul

- To act for benefit of the community without hope of reward . . . so long as ones duty as laid down by the requirement of caste is performed

- To resign oneself with absolute patience to pain and suffering and loss and feel no exultation in success"[1b]

In other words, to fit oneself for the position of a ruler one must have overcome all human weaknesses and renounced all material rewards. In a similar vein is the discussion on matters related to requirements of other castes, and as such, the above is sufficient to show that what differentiates them is simply character. He continues, stressing the fact that more than one observer has commented on the purity, regularity, equity and strictness of the ancient Indian government, "The ideal

Hindu kingdom is not an utopian dream, still exists in the hearts of Hindus, that it was based upon a social system which secured the happiness and contentment and loyalty of all classes of the people, and that the later stages of corruption and confusion have been due to foreign intrusion whether from central Asia or from Europe, whilst whatever unrest now prevails in India is caused by the incessant struggles of the Hindu caste ideal against alien influences." About the caste system existing then, he says, ". . . as a matter of fact, though we talk of upper and lower castes, no caste was originally considered superior or inferior . . . though in the Sudra the body is predominant, in the Vaisya the reason, in the Kshtriya the heart and in the Brahmin the soul, all castes are equally manifestations of Brahma though of different qualities. The relation between a higher and lower caste is then more like that between an adult and a child than that between a noble and a serf." He says further, "It provides every member of the community with a position which, though rigidly fixed, is fixed only by his natural limitations, and so allows him every opportunity of using to their full extent whatever abilities he may possess to the general advantage."

The views expressed by O P Gupta[5a] also are not dissimilar, "Supporters of caste oftenly quote two slokas viz. (IV.13) and (XVIII.41) of Shrimad Bhagwat Gita to support four castes by birth. Let us examine. In sloka (IV.13) Lord Krishna says: "Chaturvarnyma mayaa sristam gunkarma vibhagsah" i.e. four orders of society created by Me according to their Guna (qualities/behavior) and Karma (profession/work/

efforts). Lord Krishna does not say guna and karma of previous life. In sloka (XVIII.41) Lord Krishna says "Brahmana Kshatriya visham sudranam cha paramtapa, karmani pravibhaktani svabhavaprabhavaigunaih." It means people have been grouped into four classes according to their present life karma (profession/work) and svabhava (behaviour). `The division of labor into four categories—Brahman, Ksatriya, Vaishya and Sudra—is also based on the Gunas inherent in peoples' nature`. Had this division been based on birth, Lord Krishna would have naturally used phrase 'Janmani pravibhaktani' in the very shloka (XVIII.41). In sloka (XVIII.42), Lord Krishna prescribes duties (karma) which one must do in order to qualify as a Brahman i.e. among other duties (karma), he must have studied Vedas and must teach Vedas to others. Thus, if a person has neither studied Veda, nor teaches Veda to others, he is not a Brahman."

During the journeys of Hieun Tsang, he is said to have mentioned ". . . society consists of four caste groups. These four castes form classes for ceremonial purity." [5b]

Such a system, where social life is entirely independent of political government naturally disintegrated when Indian society came into contact with various invading societies, the most potent intrusion being the one beginning with the landing of Portugese adventurers at Calicut with VascoDaGama, who utilized the diversity in social positions among Indians as a convenience in governance by according political legitimacy to existing differences. These variations, which were of academic interest (if at all) in life thus far, might have been of great use to the invading group in governing the land. It is probable that the visitors made use of such expedients in its differential form, an obvious choice for greater effect, making caste differences as something of value in everyday life rather than being the unchangeable shackles of afterlife which people have been conveniently and rather philosophically leaving to fate. Endogamy as a custom might have got instituted in such a social system to safeguard the thus legitimized privileges as close to oneself as possible. The natural inclination among people of similar privileges to group together, would have amply supported this.

2.4   Ronald Inden[4] in his 'Imagined India' argues that caste is almost a creation of western efforts to orientalise their conquered subjects. Moreover, genomic studies pertaining to origins of castes have been able to identify differences in distribution of genetic material among different caste groups. Though many of those point to similar inferences, that lineages of caste groups (non tribal population) show relationship with central Asia while most of the lineages of tribal groups are from original Indian gene pool and that genes of upper caste population have greater affinity to Europeans than to Asians[7] compared to genes from lower caste population, there are many who think otherwise. Partha Majumdar et al.(ISI Calcutta)[8] reports after a comprehensive statistical analysis of data from ethnically diverse settlements of India, that, tribal and caste populations are highly differentiated and genetic histories have been considerably obliterated making it impossible to see any clear congruence of genetic affinities.

2.5   Whatever may be the case, meaning of caste changed much, from, what Charles Hill observed "No caste was originally considered superior or inferior, except in sense that its bodily type represented a more or less advanced stage in human habitations which must be, in turn, occupied by the soul"[1c] to one dividing people into, groups with different responsibilities, functions and rights, i.e., different societies altogether.

2.6   Endogamy as well as measures instituted by the invading group in governing the land might be able to put forth a rationale for development of caste, however fails in providing a reasonable explanation to the fact that we have myriad of castes, each having perceptible differences in ability when compared with one another.

3

EVOLUTION OF CASTE— A REVIEW

3.1   Whatever the shape, the evolution of caste took; it certainly resulted in a large multitude of castes, having easily discernable differences, especially in intellectual ability when compared with one another. As we have seen earlier, all the theories of formation and development of caste fail in providing a satisfactory explanation to this phenomenon.

3.2   This could have been caused by peculiar circumstances of the evolution of Indian society, mainly owing to the changes brought in by external stimuli, two of such being:

- Foreign occupation, conquests by Muslims, Europeans and the British, and lately,

- Russian revolution and the influence of communism on Indian thought.

As a result of these, caste became entrenched in Indian society, the stratification property offering much convenience in administration, each caste being a form of disciplined guild and the structural constitution of the castes proving to be a stable force in the direction of prosperity, each caste having more or less assured opportunities of earning livelihood.

It should be remembered that, caste being an idea, more so, of esoteric nature, such stratifications might have caused least consternation in everyday life, while meeting the self actualization needs (and similar top level ones in the hierarchy of human wants) of ancient Indian society. As mentioned at many places in puranic literature[1b, 3, 5a, 12], the overriding need of the people was to attain a desirable status in their next birth. Due to this reason populace at large was unconcerned about comforts of life, even in the activities involved with daily subsistence; or rather the present life itself was of secondary nature, as long as the list of reckonable deeds in each ones account is kept at a comfortably high level. Added to this is the fact that no ancient texts fail to bring out the importance of doing ones job as dictated by caste duties to attain a desirably better birth in next life. All these might have succeeded in instilling an otherwise unfathomable degree of indifference in each, such that nobody found it necessary either to force ones caste privileges or to react to the disagreeable impositions of caste.

3.3 That many parts of India, such as, parts of Himachal Pradesh, northeast including Assam and some parts of central India appear to have been having village communes, where all forms of labor were valued equally, probably points to the nonexistence of any form of caste-like discrimination[9a]. Also, it may be worth noting that, caste like divisions are found in the history of most nations, in American continent, Africa, Europe or elsewhere in Asia, some societies having complex divisions and others' relatively simple. Samurais and priests of early Japan and feudal lords of Europe are examples of social systems having stratification as well as hereditary progression, in the lines of caste system of India. Over and above this, a few among these nations could also boast of greater social inequalities manifested in institutions of slavery, a cruel practice, if not worse.

3.4 And that 'untouchability', which finds no place in Indian history, is mentioned in the history of Herodotus, "the pig is regarded among them as an unclean animal . . . are forbidden entry to any of the temples . . . and no one will give his daughter in marriage to a swineherd or take a wife from among them so that swineherds are forced to intermarry among themselves"[10], further supports this view.

3.5 In short, Indian society, which welcomed the first invader, was culturally a fully developed one having certain abstract notions of stratification, encompassing all aspects of life and society. Thus we have categories or different types of, men, women, guests, maidens, horses, dogs, cows, other things like plants, activities like sleeping, other abstractions like friends, enemies and others with further subdivisions leading to myriad of arcane classifications, each possessing unique functional attributes; caste being one such theme of classification.

Such an abstract nature of caste will be much clearer if we are to note that Hindu puranaic texts contain many instances where the moral worth of a person is shown to be having greater emphasis compared to other attributes, say caste or family background. For example, it says, "truthfulness, generosity, restraint, tapas, constant adherence to dharma—these always lead men to fruition (of their goal) and not caste nor family", or "Truthfulness, generosity, freedom from hatred, humility, kindness and tapas—he is known as Brahmana where all these are seen", also, "if these are seen in a Sudra and they do not exist in a Brahmaa, the Sudra would not be a Sudra and the Brahmana would not be a Brahmana"[12].

4

PROGRESSION OF CASTE— AN ANALYSIS

4.1   Before British: Early invasions to India, almost all, resulted in Islamic rule in India which created "a much stronger and much unified elite, which made it difficult for the ordinary masses to resist social changes, particularly in the realm of philosophical choice, religious pluralism and other personal preferences"[9b]. Notion of sexual prudery and gender separation infected Hindu households as well. "This cultural, military and political intercourse does not seem to have made any other revolutionary impact on Hindu society to alter the equitable social relations drastically"[9b].

4.2   Long before the arrival of Islam, new religious or reform movements within India opposed many of the social customs. In 6th century BC, Budhism started it. On caste system as a whole, how much of an effect Budhism could produce is not known. In fact the very nature of caste in the early days is not clearly known. For example, John W McGrindle mentions[20],

"According to Megastanes, race of India is divided into seven castes.

1   Philosophers—Only they are allowed to marry outside caste.

2   Husbandmen—They cultivate land

3   Herdsmen and hunters—They lead a wandering life

4   Tradesmen—They work in trades like weapon making

5   Fighting men

6   Overseers—They conduct general supervision and report to king

7   Assessors and councilors—They conduct justice, public matters etc

Also, in 'Inscriptions of Nepal'[21], castes are mentioned to be resulting from "the intermingling of varnas" and Vincent Smith[22] writes "Though each caste has its own dharma, the conduct is less rigid than it has been since Moslem invasions".

4.3 Effects of British ascendancy: In the beginning the British did no attempt to interfere with the caste system prevailing in India. In his observations on India, Karl Marx writes "The village isolation produced the absence of roads in India and the absence of roads perpetuated the village isolation. On this plan a community existed with a given scale of low conveniences, almost without intercourse with other villages, and without the desires and efforts indispensable to social advance"[14, 17]. The British, by bringing steam and railways into India initiated regular and rapid communication. Further introduction of roads breaking up the "self sufficient inertia" of Indian villages are some of the effects of British rule, though aimed at confiscating from India wealth in every possible form while "forbidding at the same time propagation of ideas which might not have been favorable for such ends. The modern industry resulting from railway system will dissolve the hereditary divisions of labor, upon which rests the Indian castes"[14]. But that did not take place, changes in the social atmosphere initiated by modern industry happened to get sequestered to suit the ordering of caste system.

4.4 In a paper 'The Indian caste system and the British ethnographic mapping'[15], Kevin Hobson says, "The caste system had been a fascination of the British since their arrival in India. Coming from a society that was divided by class, the British attempted to equate the caste system to the class system." As late as 1937, Professor TC Hodson stated that: 'Class and caste stand to each other in the relation of family to species. The general classification is by classes, the detailed one by castes. The former represents the external, the latter the internal view of the social organization.' The difficulty with definitions such as this is that class is based on political and economic factors, caste is not. In fairness to Professor Hodson, by the time of his writing, caste had taken on many of the characteristics that he ascribed to it in addition to the ones already attributed by his predecessors, but during the 19th century caste was not what the British believed it to be. It did not constitute a rigid description of the occupation and social level of a given group and it did not bear any real resemblance to the class system. However, this will be dealt with later in this essay.

"At present, the main concern is that the British saw caste as a way to manage a huge population by breaking it down into discrete chunks, each having specific characteristics and an inbuilt disciplinary structure. Moreover, it appears that the caste system extant in the late 19th and early 20th century has been altered as a result of British actions so that it increasingly took on the features that were ascribed to by the British. What the British failed to realize was that the Hindus existed in a different cosmological frame than did the British. The concern of the true Hindu was not his ranking economically within society but rather his ability to regenerate on a higher plane of existence during each successive life"[15]. He goes on to say "A census was undertaken in India, in 1872 for the first time, as one of the main tools used in the British attempt to understand Indian population. The census forced the Indian social system into a written schematic in a way that had never been experienced in the past. While the mughals had issued written decrees on the status of individual castes, there had never been a formal systematic attempt to organize and schedule all of the castes in an official document until the advent of the British census. The data was compiled on the British understanding of India". Based on the census results, the British formed certain notions about Indian society and "these notions led to classification of intelligence and abilities based on physical attributes and this in turn led to employment opportunities being limited to certain caste groupings that displayed the appropriate attributes. Indians attempted to incorporate themselves into this evolving system by organizing caste 'sabhas' with the purpose of attaining improved status within the system. This ran contrary to traditional purpose of caste system and imposed an economic basis. With this, the relevance and importance of the spiritual, non-material rationale for caste was degraded and caste took a far more material meaning. In a sense caste became politicized as decisions regarding caste increasingly fell into political rather than spiritual sphere of influence. With this politicization, caste moved closer to class in connotation . . . In expropriating the knowledge base of Indian society, the British had forced Indian society and caste system to execute adjustments in order to prosper within the rubric of the British regime". Thus we can see that caste was appropriated and in many respects reinvented by the British to create what it is now, with Brahman clearly at the head. That such was not the case in earlier times is mentioned, among others, by Dr Subhash Sharma[16], who says that "the evolution of the society and customs were mainly due to individual and collective needs and choices. In addition, role and influence of various espoused or suggested proclamations such as, involving 'varnasrama dharma, manusmriti', on the development and progress of society at large was rather insignificant."

5

CASTE AND NATIONALIST MOVEMENTS—AN APPRAISAL

5.1   History of India is replete with stories of social moderation efforts or other rearrangements, that too of a permanent nature, necessitated by a non homogeneous society. In the early times, if Budhism and Jainism heralded such efforts, we have Sikhism of relatively recent origin, all forerunners of social reformists. Raja Rammohan Roy, who could be called the father of Hindu reformation, gave leadership to Hindu revival in modern times. Dayanand Saraswati and Arya samaj, Annie Besant and Theosophocal society, Ramkrishna, Swami Vivekananda are some of those great ones who tried to cut through the sectarian lines of Indian religious organization, whose life and times certainly had been a source of inspiration for such efforts during freedom movement. However, those not belonging to upper castes, on becoming members realized that these organizations were primarily concerned with resurgence of Hinduism rather than reform as exemplified in the case of Swami Achyuthanand[16], one of the important scheduled caste leaders of UP in 1920-30, who was a member of Arya samaj. The untouchables and other low castes resorted to 'low caste movements' of various nature, all of which can be broadly classified into two groups, those advocating resilience of hierarchy while adopting the basic notions of caste system or those suggesting adjustments in practice of caste system to include egalitarian precepts, an exception perhaps being found in Mahatmaji's views on social struggle.

5.2   Mahatma Gandhi's views, about caste and the many facets of such social 'ills', underwent a gradual change, from 1920's to late 1940's.

- In 1920, he believed in the inevitability of caste system and that the many fruits that Indian society reaped over centuries were mainly owing to this. As examples, "I believe that caste has saved Hinduism from disintegration[18a]", or, "In accepting the fourfold division, I am accepting the laws of nature[18b]" can be quoted.

- By mid 20's, he would start downplaying the inevitability of natural division, "In my conception of the law of varna, no one is superior to any other . . . A scavenger has the same status as a Brahmin[18c]".

- As the 30's reached, he started observing that "unequal economic and social status perhaps existed, over the ages, and we have to enrich the inheritance left to us[18d]" and by 1935, "caste has to go. The sooner the public opinion abolishes it, the better[18e]".

- In 1940, he started expressing the importance of marriages between 'atishudras' and caste Hindus. From according "highest importance to marriages between atishudras and caste Hindus[18f]" and declaring that he will bless a couple "if the girl is from another community only[18g]", he reached,

- by 1945, understanding inter-caste as well as inter-religious marriage (if necessary, civil marriages), as a welcome reform, and

- by 1947, he welcomed "inter-religious marriages whenever it took place[18h]" Had it not been for his assassination, we would have been witnessing Indian society, more as Gandhiji expressed on numerous occasions, "entire Hindu society converted to my view[18i]".

5.3 The path caste took, during birth of free India and her democracy can be summed up thus: "Nevertheless, whether in relation to history of gender, the victimization of dalits, or the rise of anti Brahmin and backward caste politics, caste has worked to compromise the easy applications of national unity and civilized history. Caste has become the focus of progressive movements and of debates about the character of post colonial politics. It has also become the uncomfortable reminder that all claims about community are claims about privilege, participation and exclusion . . . caste has simultaneously preserved the patriarchy of pre-modern society and worked to sanction the continued oppression and exclusion of women in nationalist re-imaginings of the past. Caste may be the precipitate of the modern, but it is still the specter of the past[19]".

6

CASTE—MY SIDE— THE SINGULARITIES

While studying the origin of caste system, a mistake, which seems to have crept into all the theories mentioned earlier, is that no doctrine takes the philosophical plane of existence of caste (referring to caste as 'varna', an abstraction), into account.

Though some authors[23] tend to simplify this by proposing that castes are 'hardened' form of social classes (with implications such as 'the upper caste might have been formed from the existing higher classes in society'), such conjectures do not show how the abstract 'varna' metamorphosed into iniquitous 'caste'. Social classes are not founded upon occupational limitation where as castes certainly are. The class can be thought of as 'presenting the external view of social organization', and caste, 'the internal, abstract view'.

While reflecting on the practice of caste system, all seem to have been seized by certain peculiarity or individuality exhibited by one facet of its practice leading them to ignoring all other aspects. That is, almost all authors who have written about caste in India can be seen as mentioning the many and varied forms in which it does manifest, forgetting about the internal structure of caste, in which it does perpetuate. A different view, which was espoused by Gandhiji, mentions only the inner, abstract element of caste, forgetting the many unwelcome elements of its practice.

An examination of our 'puranic' texts reveals that our forefathers spent much effort in 'classification' as a primary step in learning or understanding. Thus we have all objects, animate or inanimate, all actions and other abstractions classified into esoteric groups or subgroups, each having identifiable qualities. Many methods are mentioned about stratification, say, of men and women into 'varna' based on intellectual orientation, of women into different types based on certain social nature ('Kamasutra of Vatsyayana is a detailed treatise of this), of maidens, liars, thieves and other activities of war and love, to list a few. 'Arthsastra' of 'Chanakya' contain much dissertation on such topics.[24] Nowhere in later writings or in social customs can these romantic delineations be seen as having been practiced widely. Of the myriad of themes our 'puranic' texts contain, caste alone became instituted in later social life, and this can be attributed to the 'singularities' during evolution of social life in India.

6.1   The very first singularity is philosophy or the way it is understood. For example, it (Indian philosophy in particular and others in general) treats possessions as bringing misery to man, leading therefore to a life, where, lesser the possessions, more desirable the life becomes. We, I think, do not realize that story of progress humans made so far is the story of our efforts, in adding new possessions, retaining a few or in the destruction of some. This did lead, as Marx observed earlier[14], to formation of caste as the result of 'the total lack of social intercourse' compounded by 'absence of desires and efforts indispensable to social advance'.

In fact this will be clearer if we compare the important part played by philosophy in life's progress to the role played by a spring and dashpot mechanism in a traditional mechanical system or that played by a capacitor-inductor combination in a similar electrical system, where, these arrangements help to dampen disturbances. That such mechanisms are notably absent in systems which are expected to perform beyond conventional limits, like a supersonic fighter aircraft, goes to show that the more we tolerate disturbances, the faster shall be our pace of progress.

6.2   Next singularity is the attack by various invaders, almost all of them contributing to changes in social appearance of caste system, due to, their inability in understanding Indian caste system as well as their ability in shaping caste system to suit the needs of governing the vanquished. British, though had to the longest lasting empire in India, not only did nothing to alter the existing caste equations or for social restructuring, but also made great contributions to bring the material aspect of the caste to fore. This stands in stark opposition to their efforts in the direction of welfare of aborigines and their integration in another part of British Empire, Australia, even though "several of the tribes of southern India, who were of the race 'Homo Dravida', had more in common with Australian aboriginals than their Aryan or high caste neighbours."[30] For example, "When Dr Cecil Cook was appointed Chief Protector in 1927; he was wholly unsupportive of the missions. This was partly because of the poor conditions. More importantly, Cook had a similar vision of assimilation as West Australian Chief Protector A.O. Neville. Cook supported biological assimilation. Generally by the fifth and invariably by the sixth generation, all native characteristics of the Australian aborigine are eradicated. The problem of our half-castes will quickly be eliminated by the complete disappearance of the black race, and the swift submergence of their progeny in the white[29]."

That the British found great use in Indian caste system in the governance of this country has been well acknowledged, the diversity of races in India and the presence of a powerful Mohamedan community, being found favorable to the maintenance of their rule. As caste status percolated into various benefits accruable in the material plane, the traditional meaning of caste as varna seemed to be changing, caste have started acquiring a more earthly meaning as time went by.

6.3 Another singularity took the form of Mahatma Gandhi. His views contained advices unfavorable to caste lovers, such as, "I believe in 'varnashrama' of the Vedas which is based on absolute equality of status, notwithstanding passages to the contrary elsewhere",

"The most effective, quickest, and the most unobtrusive way to destroy caste is for reformers to begin the practice with themselves" and "The higher classes will have to descend from their pedestal"[18e].

His advice to the lower caste was that they should "endeavor to merge themselves in the ocean of Hindu community" and "trust merit to command attention"[18j]. On another occasion, he is seen as proclaiming that reserving seats (for positions) is a dangerous principle. "Protection of neglected classes should not be carried to an extent which will harm them . . ." and a person after he has secured a seat in an elected body should "depend upon his intrinsic merit and popularity to secure coveted positions"[18k]. To the "castemen", on the other hand, his advice was that they "should prove that they had obliterated caste by their readiness to take up all those occupations which the 'untouchables' engaged in. Thus they should be ready to do a scavengers work . . . . The system of cleaning toilets would then be automatically transformed. In England real Bhangis were famous engineers and sanitarians . . . who had a perfectly clean way of dealing with human excreta . . . Needless to say, the Harijans will live in the same streets as others without any segregation . . ."

Given that the prestige and influence Gandhiji had at that time, above mentioned changes would have taken place, leading to a social revolution as he would have been hoping for, resulting in a generation having, greater degree of cohesion in society, upper caste much less 'upper' and lower caste none 'lower' than any other, but for the social and political changes brought in when we introduced draft constitution with certain provisions, like reservation, for dealing with caste problem. Perhaps the very adoption of the idea of reservation (without much meaningful debate[25]) by framers of constitution might have been a hasty reaction to the 'preposterous' suggestions of Gandhiji, the acceptance of which would certainly have resulted in them or their progeny (for sure) to have lost their exclusiveness (which caste status brought).

6.4 Communism offered another singularity. Our idea of caste and the way we found solutions to the problems it posed, did alter much under the influences of communism as well as the revolutions in Russia and China.

All social movements, in fact sports more than one face. What we commonly see, a group of young (and may be not so young) men and women charged with ideals and the desire to see the 'plight' of many changed for the better, is one. A group (this may be a smaller one) of 'intellectuals' who manufacture propositions convincing enough to inspire, propel and guide them in their quest, making them move forward with incessant thrust, is the other. The former is responsible for all that we welcome in a change, the alacrity, the selfless devotion of protagonists and absence of any motive or consanguineous profit other than for benefit of all. In short, in the case of communism too, those who follow the precepts are the best of humanity and the system sometimes produce good results even though the philosophy is flawed. Also, as this happened in societies already hitting the rock bottom, something favorable could be seen in every result achieved, and that might be the reason that no one noticed the contradictions it contained, till communism collapsed.

During communism in Russia[26], the famines of 1921 and 1932-33 resulted in the death of more 5 million people each (Not counting additional deaths of 7-8 million people in the violence involved with 'dekulakization' during the period 1930-37)

In China, communists adopted genetic theory 'lysenkoism'[27], a modified form of Lamarckism, one of the main beliefs of which is that, like species help each other whereas unlike species do not, in guiding state farming policy. Accordingly, Mao ordered, organization of agriculture into collectives, introduction of certain farming practices like close planting, deep plowing, non use of chemical fertilizer etc, resulting in massive fall in agricultural output giving rise to a famine on a scale never before seen in China, in the period 1958-61, resulting in the death of a staggering 30 to 40 million Chinese.

In India, 'lysenkoism' and the possibility of inheriting environmentally acquired characteristics proposed by that theory perhaps found its way into the hearts of the 'reservationists', providing them with the necessary scientific foundation to 'reservation' as a panacea for all social inequalities.

6.5 Next singularity, the most potent of all, is reservation or its euphemism, social justice. The romantic thought, of lower caste brethren being uplifted en masse, by a tiny adaptation on the part of upper caste people, must have influenced our constitution makers.

The desirable changes reservation system did bring in, and is doing so have been discussed at length, the general idea emerging from all these is that, reservation system offers many advantages to the downtrodden, marginalized sections. The only disadvantage of reservation system is that (mainly) opportunities are being curtailed for upper caste people, that is to say,

- Advantages of 'reservation' shall be to lower castes, and

- Disadvantages of 'reservation' shall be felt by upper castes

Such an idea is preposterous. Reservation system may be providing certain advantages to marginalized sections, however, some disadvantages also is their share. The most substantial of such disadvantages is that, it reduces or takes away opportunities of competition. As competition is removed from those from lower castes, they also are denied the fruits of competition, the most significant of which, as is well known, is growth, intellectual et al. This is the most severe effect of reservation. Similarly, this system may be prejudicial to upper caste people, but some benefit is also their share. If we are also to consider the fact that people of the upper castes, due to greater opportunities of competition (or opportunities for sharper competition) made available to them as a fallout of reservation, are growing further in all faculties at a faster rate, the intellectual gap between people of lower caste and those belonging to upper caste will be on the increase as generations go by, making it difficult to cohabit, at least as equal beings.

Even this could have been introduced in a manner befitting, or as an incentive to, growth. For example, 'reservations', if limited to jobs needing higher educational or academic qualifications and merit shall be forcing those lower in caste to attain greater standards in learning. To elaborate, let us say we have introduced a new system of reservation, called 'progressive justice', according to which,

- All jobs in this country are grouped into different levels; say level 1 to level 7, with level 1 needing the lowest and level 7 needing the highest entry level educational status, say level 1 needing a pass in X standard and level 7 needing the highest qualification with certain experience.

- To begin with, reservation is applied to all jobs from levels 1 to level 7 at a progressively increasing rate. That is, if, say 10% of level 1 jobs are reserved, 12% level 2, 15% level 3 and so on with level 7 showing the maximum say 30%

- After some time, say 2 years, the system is subjected to a review when level 1 jobs shall be removed from reservation. The quantum of reservation released can be added to the quota of other higher levels. That is, if 11% level 2 jobs are reserved, 15% level 3 and so on with level 7 showing the maximum say 35%.

- After some time, say another 2 years, the system is again subjected to a review when level 1 as well as level 2 jobs shall be removed from reservation. The quantum of reservation thus released can be added to other higher levels still in force. That is, if 20% level 3 jobs are reserved, 25% level 4 and so on with level 7 showing the maximum say 40%

- After some time, say another 8 years, the when this is subjected to a review there shall be no need to continue this scheme as the ends are already met.

As mentioned earlier, the desire in providing an alternative to 'wild' suggestions of Gandhiji might have blinded all reformists from seeing any such possibilities.

In a study focusing on the 'role of education in social mobility within the context of class structure' by Hiroshi Ishida et al, class origin (corresponds to respondent's father's class) and class destination (current class of respondent) are seen to have been influenced by

- Unequal access to education for different class origins. 'two forms of educational advantage to sons of professional and managerial class(read upper castes), a better access to higher levels of education and an avoidance of lower levels'.

- Allocation of class positions (of destination) influenced by class origin. "Here also, wards of highly qualified people have advantage in access to professional and managerial positions, but they also may be successful in avoiding manual positions. Conversely, wards of poorly qualified are not only excluded from professional and managerial positions, they are more likely to be recruited to manual positions." [27] (Reserving such jobs for those from low castes is, adding fuel to fire)

Effect of education on class reproduction and mobility is remarkably uniform across nations with the exception of two socialist nations, namely, Poland and Hungary, of the above mentioned study, where, more people can be seen as choosing manual and unskilled classes as destination, irrespective of class origin. In this, a major obstacle to equality of educational opportunity probably comes from the resistance of service class origin (e.g. managerial classes) to low qualifications, in addition to having access to high qualifications. While in case of lower classes, even when they were provided with access to high qualifications, as they are now, "the easy availability of low qualifications and the possibility of finding a livelihood effectively prevented them from reaching higher destinations"[27]. Also, the low classes lack the 'cultural traits' necessary for making one strive hard to gain entry into higher levels of education. Thus, as the cultural needs and desires, the fulfillment of which is the yearning of all who try to achieve better positions in life, are not fully developed in the case of lower castes, it is all the more important that this possibility of 'finding a livelihood with low qualifications' is eliminated, for education to be of use as an expedient.

6.6 Next and probably the ultimate singularity may happen sometime in the future, many (or may be few) generations from today. In his well known essay on "Biological Possibilities for the Human Species in the Next Ten Thousand Years"[28], JBS Haldane mentions of the possibility of human species "dividing into two or more branches for development of different human capacities. To me this is a terrible danger, as such species should fail to understand each other . . . and such misunderstanding can generate quarrels and even war." Such a succession though shall be befalling on all cultures, its effect on the already stratified (intellectually) Indian society shall be momentous, and we might be on that 'branch' of the 'species', where no one should be.

7

CASTE—
A SUMMARY

Caste is a relic of dark ages. It did not evolve into a modernized version naturally as we were not the real custodians of our society, having been under foreign rule for many years and those ruled over finding great use in caste, halting any such prospect. Other countries had their share of such customs which are even more shocking, like lynching or burning at stake, various entertainments of Roman Empire, all of which, evolved into something less obnoxious, as time went by. Even in recent times, some nations continued following many questionable practices and one such, in the area of eugenics, can be cited as example, where, compulsory abortion or other control over reproduction is imposed[32].

The medicine which is being tried towards amelioration of the victims of caste is reservation. It can be easily observed that we are applying that cure with no regard to its consequences, just as we followed the caste system with no regard to its ill effects. It is only logical to realize that, even regardless of that, as the cure is not working, we need to change medication.

NOTES

1 The Indian Antiquary
   a) May 1917 Caste in India, Genesis, Mechanism and Development-BR Ambedkar. This thesis describes the role of caste system in establishing the customs of 'sati', 'girl marriage' as well as perpetuation of widowhood et al. in Hindu society.
   b) March 1930 Origin of the Caste system in India (part I)—S Charles Hill
   c) April 1930 Origin of the Caste system in India (part II)—S Charles Hill
   d) October 1930 Origin of the Caste system in India (part III)— S Charles Hill

2 An Introduction to Sociology
   DR Sachdeva and Vidya Bhushan

3 'Hindu caste system and Hinduism—vedic vocations were not related to heredity'—Dr Subhash C Sharma
   www.geocities.com/lamberdar/_caste.html

4   Quoted in 'Caste race and sociologists'
    Gail Omvedt

5   a) Caste and Bhagawat Gita—O P Gupta, IFS
        http://sify.com/news/othernews/fullstory.
        php?id=13167991
    b) http://www.palikanon.com/

6   'Origins of Castes and Tribes in India'
    R Cordaux et al. Current Biology 2004 14:231

7   'Molecular Anthropology' M Bamshad et al.
    http://jorde-lab.genetics.utah.edu/elibrary/
    Babshad_2001a.pdf

8   'Ethnic India—A Genomic view with special
    reference to peopling and structure' Partha P
    Majumdar, Anabala Basu et al.
    ISI Calcutta etc

9   'Caste and gender equations in Indian history'
    a) http://india_resource.tripod.com/social.htm
    b) http://india_resource.tripod.com/sahistory.htm

10 'The history of Herodotus', Book I CLIO
    Translated by George Rawlinson
    http://classics.mit.edu/Herodotus/history.html

11 'Battle for Liberation, Then and Now'
    Annie Namala and Paul Divakar www.labourfile.
    org, a treatise tracing the efforts in rehabilitation
    of scavengers over the years. It mentions that,
    'Narada smriti', though enumerates 15 kinds of

slaves including those engaged in disposal of human excreta; there is no reference to untouchability.

12 History of Dharmasastra

13 'The race war' Ronald Seghal Jonathan Cape 1966

14 'The future results of British rule in India' Karl Marx, New York Daily Tribune 8 August 1853 www.marxists.org/archive/marx/works/1853/07/22. htm

15 'The Indian caste system and the British— Ethnographic mapping and the construction of the British census in India' Kevin Hobson www.infinityfoundation.com/ ECITcastebritishframeset.htm

16 Mentioned at http://kellog.nd.edu/events/pdfs/ Jaffrelot.pdf

17 This could explain how endogamy came to be instituted in Indian society. Absence of roads perpetuating village isolation, the only way to ensure continuation of species might have been adopted, endogamy. That such isolation affected our society, in more ways than one, can be seen, in the interesting fact that even in 19th century kerala, those who cross river 'Bharatapuzha' were liable for excommunication, or from observing that one of the significant sources of state's income (in Kerala) was tax imposed on men of lower caste for sporting a moustache.

18 'Mahatma Gandhi, the collected works' Delhi(58-94)
   a) Vol XIX p 83
   b) Vol XXIX p 410
   c) Vol XXXV p 260
   d) Vol LIX p 319
   e) Vol LXII p 121
   f) Vol LXXX p 77
   g) Vol LXXX p 99
   h) Vol LXIV p 35
   i) Vol LXLI p 318
   j) Vol LVIII p 163
   k) Vol LXXVI p 314

A detailed study, tracing 'the change in Gandhi's ideas about varna and intermarriage over the years' is "HOW GANDHI CAME TO BELIEVE CASTE MUST BE DISMANTLED BY INTER MARRIAGE"
   • Prof Mark Lindley
     http://www.bfg-muenchen.de/caste.htm

19 Caste as India
   http://press.princeton.edu/chapters/s7191.html

20 'Ancient India as described by Megastanese and Arrian'
   John W McGrindle(Retired principal Patna college)

21 'Inscriptions of Nepal' DR Rajmi

22 'Asoka—His history' Vincent Smith

23 'Caste class and race' Oliver Cromwell Cox

24 Had this propensity for classification been continuing as such, much contribution could have been from Indian culture, towards learning, to note one possibility. Like many of the scientific terms that we use announcing the cultural heritage of the Greek, we could have been seeing similar terms in lot many areas, broadcasting the virtues of Indian civilization.

25 constituent assembly debates http://parliamentofindia.nic.in/ls/debates/vol7p3b. htm Pandit Thakur Dass Bhargava: opposes reservation during the debates while discussing art 294 of Indian constitution. ".... it may be said that in wealth, social influence and social status they are inferior, but all the same I want that their position may be leveled up in ways other than by reservation of seats . . . will be very harmful . . ." http://parliamentofindia.nic.in/ls/debates/vol9p17b. htm Shri Brajeshwar Prasad: ". . . The problems (the scheduled castes face) are primarily educational and of an economic character. They are of a cultural character. We want to raise the cultural level of these down-trodden and oppressed people. I do not see how their representation in the legislatures will in any way alter the material and the moral level of these people. Representations here and there will provide opportunities for a handful of leaders but it will not in any way materially alter their economic or their educational level. Better lay down in the Constitution that a fixed percentage in the budget, both Central and Provincial, shall be exclusively

devoted for their welfare . . . I am quite clear in my own mind that by giving them a few seats here and there, their economic condition and their education level will in no way be improved".

26 http://www.overpopulation.com/faq/health/hunger/famine

The Soviet Famines of 1921 and 1932-3 Ukrainian agronomist, Trofim D. Lysenko, well known for 'scientific declarations' regarding the perniciousness of genetics. In the U.S.S.R. of the 1930s, Trofim D. Lysenko rose to considerable power by claiming that his version of genetics, rather than that of Mendel and Darwin, could assist in the development of socialist ideology. If each successive generation of citizens had to be educated in Marxist ideology, he claimed, the utopia they envisioned would take too long to be realized. Rather, Lysenko rejected Mendelian heredity as bourgeois, and interpreted Marx as stating that man and nature are improvable and perfectible. He claimed, for example, that winter wheat could be changed to a spring variety simply by altering the temperature at which it was grown, and that, by similar means, he could change wheat into rye. Darwin's struggle for existence, too, was dismissed as a bourgeois tool used to justify competition-based capitalist society. His erroneous assertions dominated Soviet biology for 30 years. He was eventually ousted, in 1965, due to rampant crop failures and shortages. Lysenkoism has come to represent the devastating consequences of marrying science to ideology.

http://www.galafilm.com/afterdarwin/english/glossary/lysenkoism.html,
http://www.genetics.org/cgi/reprint/165/1/1.pdf,
http://www.softpanorama.org/Skeptics/lysenkoism.shtml

27 Hiroshi Ishida, Walter Müller, and John M. Ridge. 1995. "Class Origin, Class Destination, and Education: A Cross-National Study of Ten Industrial Nations". American Journal of Sociology 101: 145-193.

28 "Biological Possibilities for the Human Species in the Next Ten Thousand Years" J. B. S. Haldane
http://www.transhumanism.org/resources/Haldanebioposs.htm
One possibility mentioned in this essay is production of a human clone, which, of course, has already taken place.

29 Bringing them home—The History
http://www.hreoc.gov.au/bth/text_versions/map/history/nt.html

30 Race, Caste and Tribe in Central India: the early origins of Indian anthropometry—Crispin Bates
http://www.csas.ed.ac.uk/fichiers/BATES_RaceCaste&Tribe.pdf

31 Cultural Anthropology Felix M Keesing,
The aborigines have an intricate classification system that defines kinship relations and regulates marriages, men and women grouped as Banaka, Burung, Karimera and Palyeri. Rules of marriage,

descent, and residence determine how these sections interact: Karimera men must marry Palyeri women, and their children are Burung, Banaka men must marry Burung women and their children are Karimera and so on. The complex system, by requiring each man to marry a woman from only one of the three possible sections, fosters a broad network of social relations and creates familial solidarity within the horde as a whole.

Here, caste groupings play an important role in selecting partners in a way appropriate for inhibiting progression of many forms of illness where heredity plays a part. (It is possible that, in India too, such a property of caste can manifest, do selection of marriage partners only from outside ones caste!)

32 Civilizations can be judged by how they treat women, children, old people, and strangers. Vulnerable people bring out the kindness in every society and also the cruelty. Every so often, they become the object of practices so vile that they will cause people to recoil in horror across the centuries. One such practice is forced abortion, another is forced sterilization.

The world has known for well over 15 years now that the Government of China routinely compels women to abort their unauthorized unborn children and that the Chinese men and women are often forcibly sterilized. see http://commdocs.house.gov/ committees/intlrel/hfa49740.000/hfa49740_0.HTM The recent development of molecular genetics has created concern that society may experience a new eugenics. This paper argues that the dominant view of eugenics as morally and scientifically illegitimate is not tenable when it comes to the uses of compulsion, political motivation, and scientific acceptability. In spite of a general condemnation of eugenics, health authorities today are trying to prevent individuals with deviant behavior from reproducing or at least from rearing children. See http://journals.cambridge. org/action/displayAbstract;jsessionid=D32EE0B42B A9215764FCF0CAC4F9A7E6.tomcat1?fromPage=o nline&aid=255383